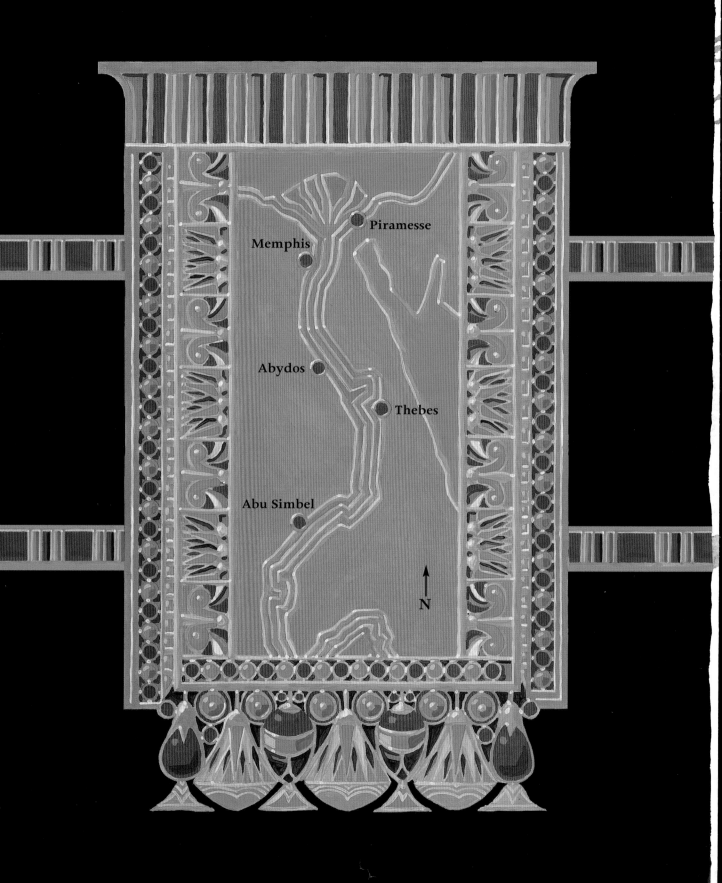

PHARAOH

Life and Afterlife of a God

For Dyan Blacklock, whose idea this was

Acknowledgments

Thanks to the May Gibbs Trust for a 2004 fellowship,
to Eija Murch-Lempinen and Celia Jellett for months of work on
this project, and to Yoshie Furusawa for keeping a close eye
on me and these pictures.

The illustrations in this book represent only about half of the
number of paintings completed over the three years that went
into producing *Pharaoh*. Inspiration and reference came from
many sources: old and contemporary photographs, television
documentaries, films, *National Geographic* magazine, and the
work of other artists—Angus McBride, Mark English, and
Bernie Fuchs, among others.

—D. K.

First published in Australia in 2008 by Omnibus Books,
an imprint of Scholastic Australia Pty Ltd
Published in the United States of America in 2008 by Walker Publishing Company, Inc.
Distributed to the trade by Holtzbrinck Publishers

For information about permission to reproduce selections from this book, write to
Permissions, Walker & Company, 175 Fifth Avenue, New York, New York 10010

Library of Congress Cataloging-in-Publication Data
Kennett, David.
Pharaoh : life and afterlife of a God / David Kennett. — 1st ed.
      p.   cm.
Previously published: Australia : Omnibus Books, 2008.
ISBN-13: 978-0-8027-9567-0 • ISBN-10: 0-8027-9567-6 (hardcover)
ISBN-13: 978-0-8027-9568-7 • ISBN-10: 0-8027-9568-4 (library binding)
1. Pharaohs—Juvenile literature. 2. Pharaohs—Religious aspects—Juvenile literature.
I. Title.
DT61.K443 2008   932—dc22   2007024236

Visit Walker & Company's Web site at www.walkeryoungreaders.com

Typeset in Apollo, Didot, and Venis
Art created with acrylic paint

Printed in Malaysia by Tien Wah Press Ltd.
10 9 8 7 6 5 4 3 2 1 (hardcover)
10 9 8 7 6 5 4 3 2 1 (library binding)

PHARAOH
Life and Afterlife of a God

In ancient Egypt, Seti I, the pharaoh, is the supreme ruler and holder of all power—a living god. It is through Pharaoh that the Egyptian people know the will of the gods. Keeping their gods happy is the best way the Egyptians can keep their world safe. It is Pharaoh's duty to raise lasting monuments—glories in stone—that celebrate the gods and remind the people of their religion.

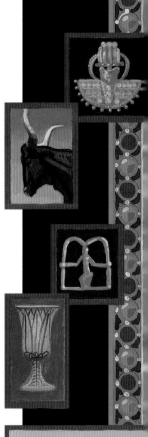

Historians divide ancient Egyptian history into three periods—the Old Kingdom (circa 2649–2040 BC), the Middle Kingdom (circa 2040–1550 BC), and the New Kingdom (circa 1550–1070 BC). Seti I is a king of the New Kingdom. He has been preparing for his death since the day he became pharaoh, thirteen years earlier. When he dies, his son Ramesses II will rule in his place, becoming one of Egypt's most famous pharaohs.

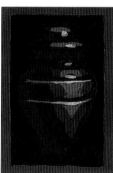

When Seti I dies in 1290 BC, the next stage of his journey toward everlasting life can begin. Embalming Seti's body takes seventy days. The body is dried with a naturally occurring salt called natron. Vital organs are removed. The body is washed and filled with resin and bundles of linen, then wrapped in great lengths of linen bandages and protective amulets. Next, the wrapped body is put into a nest of mummy cases covered in magical spells and

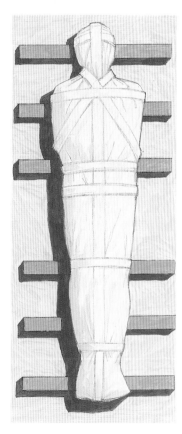

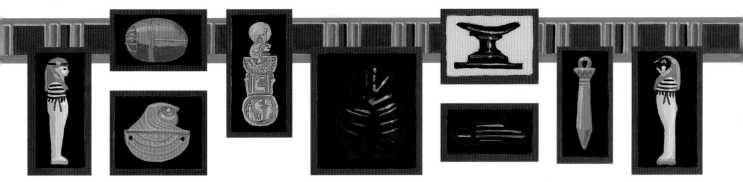

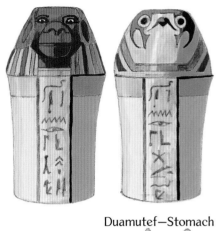

Hapy—Lungs

Qebehsenuef—Intestines

protective artwork. The lungs, intestines, liver, and stomach, which have been removed from the body, are preserved and stored separately in containers called canopic jars, each specially decorated with a god to protect a particular organ. The box holding the canopic jars is placed inside a richly decorated and gilded shrine protected by four goddesses: Isis, Nephtys, Neith, and Selkis.

Embalming is an industry in ancient Egypt. Embalmers wrap not only people but also animals. There are hundreds of animal-headed gods resembling birds, reptiles, and insects. Egyptians believe that offering the mummified remains of a creature to the god that represents it will grant them favor with that god.

Imsety—Liver

Duamutef—Stomach

Many years ago, during the time of the Old Kingdom, pharaohs were buried in great pyramids. New Kingdom pharaohs, like Seti I, are buried in the Valley of the Kings, near Thebes. This religious center lies at a midpoint between the fertile Nile delta to the north and bustling Nubia to the south. The pharaoh's many wives are also buried nearby, in the Valley of the Queens.

Seti's mummy has been resting in the care of the god Osiris in the temple Seti built at Abydos. Now, after its journey by barge on the river to the Valley of the Kings, it is ready for burial. It lies in a boat-shaped bier on a sled decorated with flowers and pulled by oxen. A priest walks ahead, burning incense and sprinkling milk on the ground. Other priests follow Seti's mummy, dragging the canopic shrine with the pharaoh's organs. Professional mourners dressed in pale blue are crying, throwing dirt on themselves, and tearing at their hair. Soldiers keep the crowds at bay along the route. The entrance to the Valley of the Kings is closely guarded, and only the funeral party is allowed to pass through to the site of Seti's tomb, where the final rituals will be performed.

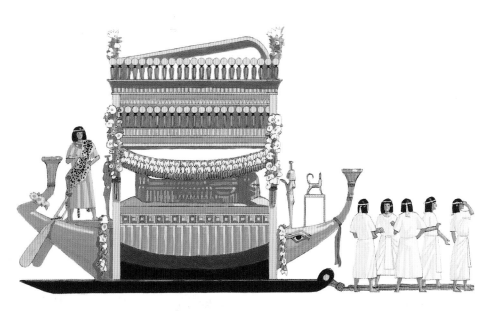

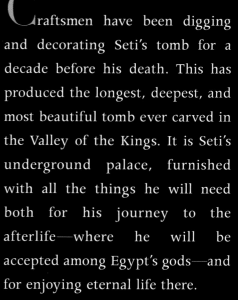

Craftsmen have been digging and decorating Seti's tomb for a decade before his death. This has produced the longest, deepest, and most beautiful tomb ever carved in the Valley of the Kings. It is Seti's underground palace, furnished with all the things he will need both for his journey to the afterlife—where he will be accepted among Egypt's gods—and for enjoying eternal life there.

At the tomb, Seti's mummy is purified with water, incense, and natron. Sacred oils are applied. The most important ceremony is "the opening of the mouth." It will restore Seti's senses so that he can be reborn in the afterlife. His son Ramesses conducts the ritual, which involves touching Seti's mummy with magical implements in seventy-five separate acts. Other priests recite funerary texts.

Seti's mummy is placed in his alabaster sarcophagus. A series of nested, gilded shrines is erected around it. Lamps are lit and the funeral party retires, leaving Seti to continue his journey in silence. The tomb is sealed, and the living hold a feast in Seti's honor.

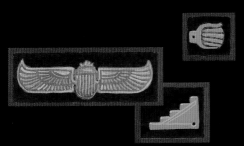

Egyptians believe the afterlife is a paradise, pictured in many tomb paintings as the river Nile and its fertile green fields and marshlands. During the nighttime hours, they believe the sun journeys underground, where it is threatened by terrible dangers. The soul of Seti faces a similar journey. To help Pharaoh overcome these dangers, the Book of the Dead, a collection of more than two hundred spells (or chapters), provides information on every aspect of the soul's journey to rebirth in paradise.

Scribes write out the spells onto rolls of papyrus, which are placed with the mummy in the tomb. Spells can also be written on coffins, amulets, tomb walls, and statues.

1. The soul (Ka) of Seti is "taken under the wing" of the goddess Isis.

2. Isis entrusts the soul to the god Anubis. This wise and compassionate god will guide and comfort on the journey ahead.

3. Anubis and Seti's soul go to the world's end and cross over one of the mountains that hold up the sky.

4. They go down into the "gallery of the night" and navigate their boat through endless rapids.

5. There are many dangers on this journey. On the riverbank, giant baboons try to capture them in a great net.

6. Knife-carrying snakes attack them. They must recite a spell to protect themselves.

7. Dragons spit fire at them. There is a spell to protect against these creatures as well.

8. To pass through the seven gates and out of this place, they must know the magical words and secret name of each gate's guardian—fearsome names such as "Swallower of Sinners" or "Existing on Maggots."

9. They pass through ten pylons. At each pylon in turn, a god reveals to Seti a secret name.

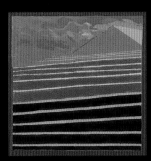

10. Coming at last to the hall of Osiris, filled with the gods of the universe, they climb the "staircase of justice."

11. At the top of the pyramid staircase are the four gods, the high judges who created the world.

    Shu (Air)
    Bastet (Fire)

12. Geb (Earth)
    Nut (Sky)

    The gods wait there to meet the soul of Seti and the god Anubis.

13. Now the soul faces Osiris, god of the underworld, for final judgment. It declares its innocence to each of the gods: to the Blood Eater it says, *I have not killed a sacred bull;* to the Swallower of Shades, *I have not stolen;* to the Bone Breaker, *I have not lied.*

14. The god Thoth is ready to note the outcome of the "weighing of the heart." Thoth is the god of learning and of writing, and he is therefore associated with scribes.

15. The demoness Ammut is part crocodile, part hippopotamus, and part lion. It will eat the soul if it fails the heart-weighing test. To stop the heart from revealing past sins, spells to keep it silent are written on the underside of the heart scarab.

16. Anubis places Seti's heart in one pan of the scales. The feather of truth is in the other. The heart and the feather must be in balance.

17. The redeemed soul purifies itself in the lotus lake. All earthly cares and concerns are washed away.

18. The soul is now young and pure, and it begins its everlasting life working in the fields of paradise. It is reunited with loved ones who died before.

Egypt is a world full of magic, and in a magical world all things are possible. During his reign as pharaoh, Seti is considered part god, part man—the bridge between the world of humans and the world of gods. In death he becomes fully divine, a true god. Seti is a king in the afterlife just as he was in this world.

On earth, Ramesses is now pharaoh of Egypt. His coronation has made him part man and part god.

Ramesses is now the chief priest of Egypt. He has daily and seasonal rituals to perform that are vital to the preservation of Ma'at (order). Ramesses performs the dawn ceremony to help the sun rise every morning, as the sun is vital to a society that depends on farming crops.

Egypt's gods live among the people, and as the people's most important and powerful beings, they need splendid homes to live in. Pharaoh gives the temples large tracts of land. These estates grow crops and raise animals. All the produce and livestock flow into the temples, where they are measured, recorded, stored, and distributed.

The career of a priest offers wealth, power, and prestige. Only a few priests perform religious rituals. Others run the temple workshops, storerooms, and libraries. Astronomer priests compile the festival calendar. In the "House of Life," priests teach reading and writing and copy manuscripts for the library. In the community, they work as scribes, writing up documents such as wills and divorce settlements.

Ramesses chooses the high priest. Below him are two classes of priests: high-ranking, full-time, professional priests, or lector priests; and lower-ranked, part-time priests called wab priests. The high priest and his assistants are allowed to serve the god image directly; the lower priests are not. Female priests are often the cult singers, dancers, and musicians.

Priests are paid in land grants from the temple estate and by rations of the daily food offerings.

Karnak, on the bank of the Nile to the east of the Valley of the Kings, is the largest temple complex ever built. Amun, the patron god of Thebes, is worshipped here. The complex was begun by an earlier pharaoh and added to by Seti and Ramesses. Statues of Ramesses sit before the entrance. The outside walls are decorated with scenes of the military campaigns of Seti and Ramesses.

A series of pylons marks each entrance into the temple area. Before entering the temples, priests purify themselves by washing in the sacred lake. The lake is home to flocks of geese, which are sacred to the god Amun. Priests live in houses within the temple walls or close by in the districts outside.

The design, construction, and decoration of Egyptian temples reflect the flood cycle of the river Nile. The main hall at Karnak has 134 gigantic papyrus-shaped columns, walls decorated with scenes of reed beds, and a floor polished to a watery sheen to resemble the land during flood season. When the river does rise and overflow, the outer courts of some temples may actually flood.

The floor levels of the temple's inner sanctuaries, where the image of the god is tended by the elite among the priesthood, are higher than those of the outer courts to keep them dry at all times.

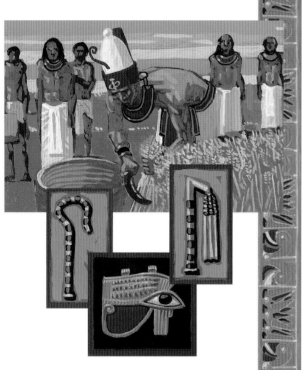

Flooding by the river Nile is actually a necessity in Egypt—when the waters recede, they leave a renewed, rich black soil that allows for better farming. Sometimes, however, the flood waters rise too high and threaten people's livelihoods. When this happens, the people look to their pharaoh for solace. Since he is their living representation of the gods, he is expected to intercede with the gods on their behalf in times of trouble. The lives of Egypt's rural people are hard and often short. Magic is the only protection against disease and illness, and they wear at least one magical amulet to keep them safe. They build mud-brick houses above the line of the annual flood, but these can be swept away if the water rises too high.

Pharaoh is a source of religious inspiration, but he is also in charge of the practicalities of everyday living in Egypt. The condition of Egypt's farmland and the functioning of the canal system are among Ramesses' chief concerns. He attends agricultural festivals and ceremonies to ensure good floods, sowing, and harvests. He also cuts the first sheaf of grain at harvest time.

Just as Egyptian lives are dependent on Pharaoh's divine intervention and daily

leadership, Pharaoh's livelihood and success are dependent on the success of the villagers' farming.

Farmers' techniques throughout Egypt are generally the same. They scatter seed corn by hand, with a herd of sheep or goats following behind to trample the seed into the ground. It is the children's job to scare away the birds from the newly sprouted grain. When the grain is ready, it is harvested and taken to the threshing floor. Cattle or donkeys trample over it until the seed comes free of the case. The grain is measured and kept in hive-shaped stores of mud brick to keep it safe from rats and mice.

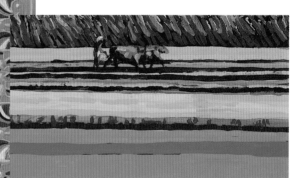

Most Egyptians live along the green ribbon of cultivated land beside the river Nile that stretches from the delta in the north to the border of Nubia in the south.

All types of boats can be seen on the Nile. There are huge barges transporting building stone from the quarries, trading ships carrying goods from distant parts of the empire and beyond, fishing boats and ferries to take people back and forth across the river, warships and oceangoing vessels, and sacred barges to transport the temple gods during festivals.

The river is a lush place of reeds and wetlands, which are home to an abundance of waterbirds, fish, insects, and animals such as hippopotamuses and crocodiles.

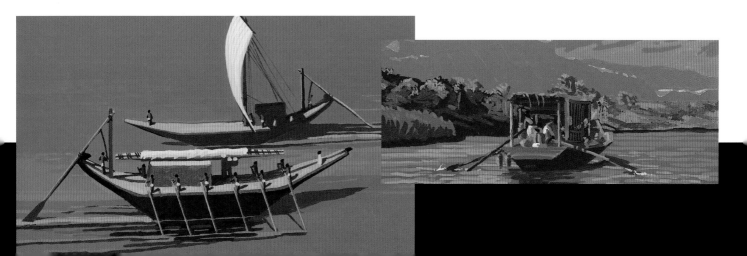

oyal barges take Pharaoh and his court up and down the length of the Nile on business or to set up court at one of the many palaces dotting the land. All along the Nile are cities large and small—great religious and cultural centers such as Thebes, Memphis, and Abydos, or the new capital city Ramesses is building in the delta, Piramesse.

Because of their location on the river Nile, many cities in Egypt deal primarily in trading goods with other countries. The import-and-export business is a monopoly run by Ramesses' administration. Egypt exports many natural resources, including grain, gold, copper, malachite, gemstones, minerals, and natron. It also imports many items from its neighboring countries, including timbers from Lebanon for construction, and copper, oil, aromatic wood, resin, ointments, wine, opium, and manufactured goods from the eastern Mediterranean.

The temples are central to Egypt's domestic economy and are heavily involved in trade. The temple of Amun at Karnak has a fleet

of eighty-three ships trading in the Mediterranean, and agents for the temples operate in foreign ports.

Towns like Siwa are important centers on the oasis route in and out of Nubia and the Sudan. Nubia is a land rich in gold, ivory, ebony, incense, ostrich plumes, cattle, animal skins, and aromatic woods. Traveling the Nile from the delta to the Nubian border takes three weeks. There are trade routes linking Egypt to the Red Sea, and fast ships sailing from the Aegean Sea can be in Egypt in five days.

Even while the pharaoh is busy overseeing everyday life in Egypt, he is always mindful of his eventual move into the afterlife and his transition into a god. His temples will be his legacy. Therefore, their construction is of the utmost importance to him, and much of the profits he makes from trade go toward their construction.

Thousands of workers are now employed to build Ramesses' huge mortuary temple, the Ramesseum in western Thebes, to house Pharaoh after his death. Produce from the floodplain is stored in its many vaulted storerooms for eventual distribution throughout the society.

The temple's magnificence is a symbol of the pharaoh's triumphs during his rule. So, in addition to building their own temples, pharaohs will often enlarge and beautify existing temples in an attempt to compete with and outdo earlier rulers. They will sometimes even obliterate their predecessors' hieroglyphic inscriptions and replace them with their own. Ramesses has his craftsmen cut his glyphs deep into the stone to stop this from happening to him.

In contrast to the splendor of the pharaoh's temple, other royal palaces and workers' houses are made largely of mud brick. In a desert climate, mud-brick houses are cooler than those made of stone. Workers' houses have small windows set high in the walls and air vents in the roofs to allow hot air to escape and cool evening breezes to come in. The roofs are flat so people can sleep outside on them on hot summer nights.

Egyptians are master builders. They use ramps of mud brick and sand to build the huge pylons and columns of the temples. Columns are made by stacking roughly shaped disks of stone, which are smoothed and shaped with chisels. They are then carved and painted from the top down. A newly raised pylon or column can be nearly buried by the ramp and platform used in its construction. This is gradually removed as craftsmen complete each section.

Egyptian stonemasons can choose from many varieties of stone to work with, most from quarries in Egypt. Sandstone is often used for constructing temples, although its softness requires that roof spans are kept short and supporting columns close together. Harder stone like granite and basalt is used for statues, floors, and pavements.

The Valley of the Kings is known as the "Great Place." The Medjay, a Nubian police force, guard the valley—not only the treasures buried in the royal tombs but also the warehouses full of workers' supplies. The tomb workers and their families have a better living standard than other Egyptian workers. Their village is in the desert in western Thebes, close to the Ramesseum, which provides them with food, water, lamp oil, and other materials.

The images that the tomb artists make are not

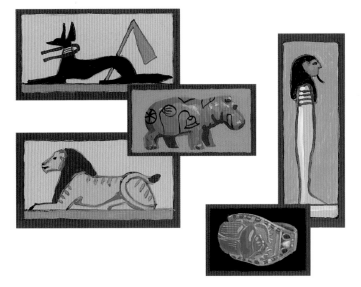

just decorations. Images and models of everything Pharaoh has enjoyed are placed in his tomb, and priests bring them to life with special rituals so that he can enjoy them in the afterlife.

It is important that the workers build Pharaoh's tomb quickly and efficiently so that at least some rooms will be finished if he happens to die unexpectedly. Because of this, workers will usually alternate the excavation of the rooms with the decorating of the interior, finishing certain rooms before continuing on to others.

Although most Egyptians are farmers, many others find work as artists and craftsmen. They are kept busy making furniture, clothes, tools, boats, jewelry, sculptures, and pottery for Ramesses and his court. Some of these items, such as sandals or baskets, are used by everyone, whereas others, such as the delicate and beautiful jewelry, are worn only by Ramesses and the royal family.

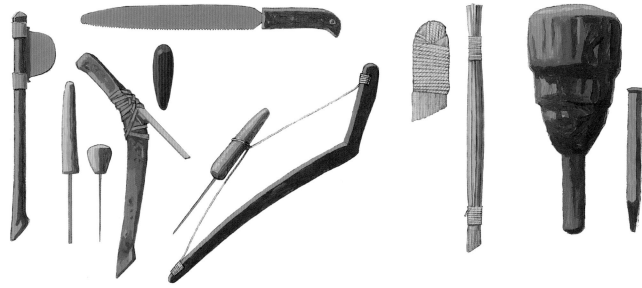

Although Ramesses is all-powerful, he is not able to oversee every order of business at once. Therefore, the daily business of the empire is dealt with by the bureau of the viziers. They are Ramesses' top officials and report to him regularly. The positions are hereditary and are taken by members of the ruling family.

Because of its viziers and trade economy, Egypt is a dominant power in the Middle East. Its sophisticated culture spreads far and wide, and foreigners come to Egypt as traders and artisans or as part of diplomatic missions. Children from foreign courts are fostered here, and people also come simply as tourists.

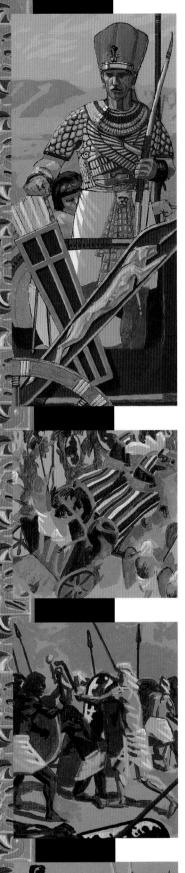

Although many countries revere Egypt for its power and beauty, from time to time it does enter into a state of war with its neighboring countries. Ramesses is skillful in the art of war, and he is trained in battle strategy and tactics. He can handle ships and is the leader of his premier fighting unit, the chariot corps. There are auxiliary troops in his army along with the regular Egyptian nationals. These other units come from the neighboring countries of Syria, Canaan, Nubia, and Libya.

There is no separate navy in the Egyptian military. Instead, it is an integral part of the army and is often used to transport troops to Nubia or the Middle East. Nubia is an important source of gold for Ramesses, and his vast building programs require a steady supply. The navy is essential in keeping Nubia under Egyptian control.

Maintaining a permanent army requires a lot of organization to ensure that there are enough weapons, chariots, horses, and ships to equip that army. State workshops produce weapons and armor, and the dockyard at Memphis builds ships. The state provides stud farms and grazing land for horses so that the chariot corps has enough horsepower to meet its needs.

Military scribes record all aspects of army life, and the whole military bureaucracy is under the watchful eye of Ramesses' military vizier. Egypt's administrative genius has made it a feared military power, a Bronze Age superpower.

Memphis

Piramesse

Abydos

Thebes

Abu Simbel

N

In order to assert their higher status and power, the men and women of Ramesses' court wear heavy wigs, makeup, and jewelry. A wig rests on a thick pad that allows some air to circulate between it and the scalp, to keep the wearer cool. Egyptians keep their own hair short or shaved, to control head lice. Eye paint and other cosmetics are made from powdered minerals mixed with animal fat.

Egyptian craftsmen make fine jewelry from gold and alloys. Stones are chosen for color: red carnelian from the eastern desert, blue-green turquoise from Sinai, and deep blue lapis lazuli from Afghanistan.

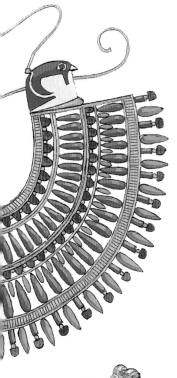

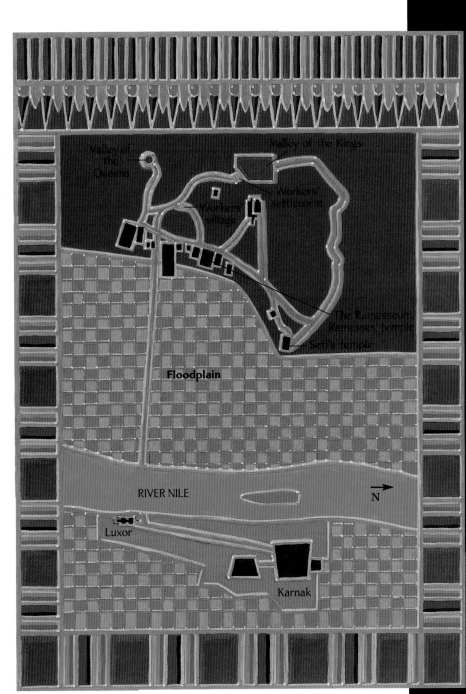

Valley of the Queens

Valley of the Kings

Workers' settlement

Workers' village

The Ramesseum, Ramesses' temple

Seti's temple

Floodplain

RIVER NILE

N

Luxor

Karnak

Goldsmiths are a privileged group who work mostly in royal or temple workshops. Gold and silver are hammered with polished stones and filed with abrasive stones. A bow drill is used for making holes, its copper point aided by abrasive powder such as crushed flint or quartz sand. There are also precious-stone workers, faience makers, and necklace and bead makers. Beads made of faience do not need drilling because they are molded around a thread that burns away during firing, leaving a hole. Earrings and ear studs can be heavy and very large. Bracelets, arm rings, anklets, finger rings, girdles, and belts are all common.

Not only does Ramesses' jewelry show his wealth and status, but his appearance symbolizes his role as the ruler of all Egypt. The symbols of Pharaoh's power are the stylized shepherd's crook and the grain flail, an agricultural tool that is used during the harvest. Ramesses wears one of several crowns to symbolize different aspects of his divinity: one crown each for upper and lower Egypt and one crown to unite them, a blue crown for war, and the crown of Osiris.

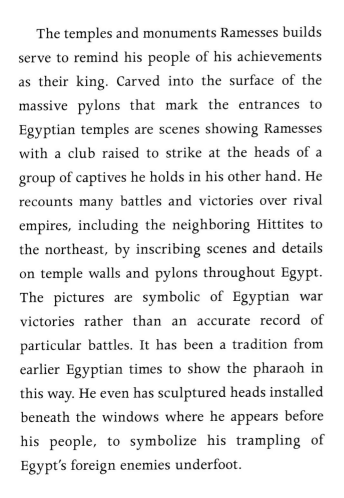

The temples and monuments Ramesses builds serve to remind his people of his achievements as their king. Carved into the surface of the massive pylons that mark the entrances to Egyptian temples are scenes showing Ramesses with a club raised to strike at the heads of a group of captives he holds in his other hand. He recounts many battles and victories over rival empires, including the neighboring Hittites to the northeast, by inscribing scenes and details on temple walls and pylons throughout Egypt. The pictures are symbolic of Egyptian war victories rather than an accurate record of particular battles. It has been a tradition from earlier Egyptian times to show the pharaoh in this way. He even has sculptured heads installed beneath the windows where he appears before his people, to symbolize his trampling of Egypt's foreign enemies underfoot.

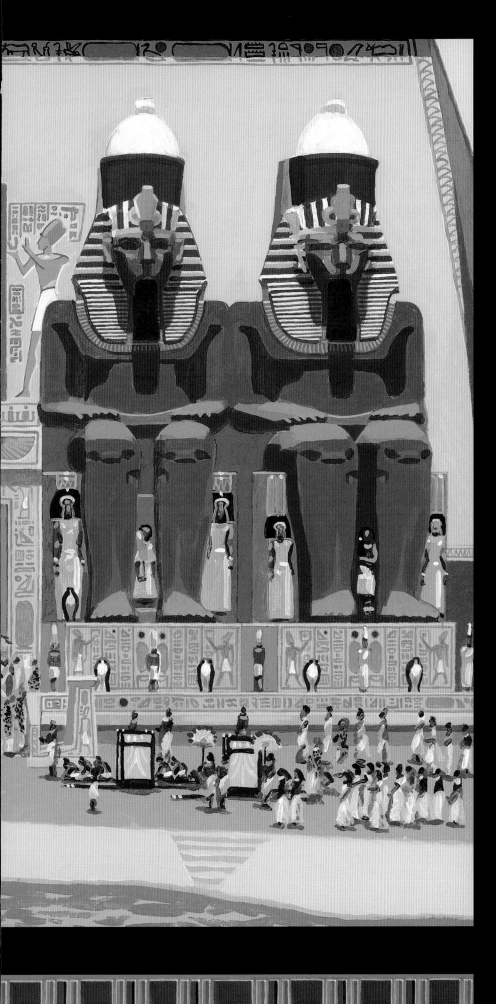

In addition to waging war with neighboring countries, Egypt is strong enough to colonize countries rich in goods that are beneficial to its economy. Nubia, the country to the south of Egypt, is under Egyptian control. Seti I developed gold mines in Nubia, and Ramesses continues to exploit them. By building temples, he seeks to remind the local tribespeople that Egypt is master.

The greatest of these temples is at Abu Simbel, where the temple is cut 66 yards (60 meters) into the cliff face and looks out onto the Nile. At the front of the large temple sit four huge statues of Pharaoh. On certain days in February and October, the rising sun aligns with the temple entrance and the interior floods with light.

A smaller temple nearby is built in honor of Pharaoh's wife Nefertari (*Nefer* is Egyptian for "beautiful"). Both of these temples are begun early in Ramesses' reign and dedicated in his twenty-fourth year as pharaoh. Nefertari has little time to enjoy this tribute, as she dies the following year. Pharaoh also has a large number of other wives and concubines and many children.

Ramesses rules Egypt for sixty-seven years, and during this time the workers in the "Great Place" are constructing and decorating his tomb. Such a long reign means that over time, the artisans scale back their activities, working fewer days and reducing their numbers. With more free time, the workers lavish attention on their own tombs. Some of the most beautiful personal tombs in the village necropolis date from the reign of Ramesses II.

Workers not needed on Ramesses' tomb are sent to work in the Theban temples and to cut tombs in the Valley of the Queens for other members of the royal family. The beautiful tomb of Ramesses' queen Nefertari is in this valley.

All pharaohs are living gods, but few fit the title as well as Ramesses II. He strides as largely as any of his colossal statues across the landscape of Egypt's history. But we see Ramesses' Egypt as if through a sandstorm, with many tantalizing details obscured by time. Nevertheless, he was and will always remain Ramesses the Great.

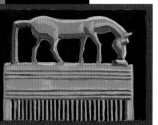

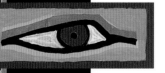

GLOSSARY

afterlife • life after death

alabaster • white stone often used to make coffins

amulet • charm to protect against evil

bier • framework supporting a coffin on its way to burial

Book of the Dead • collection of protective spells, usually written on papyrus, placed with the dead to help the soul to the afterlife

canopic jars • urns that contain the preserved organs of an embalmed body

chariot corps • the premier fighting unit in the Egyptian army

concubine • woman who is part of a king's household but not married to him

delta • triangular area at the mouth of a river with deposits of earth that divide the river into smaller streams

ebony • heavy, hard dark wood

embalm • preserve a dead body using chemicals

faience • ceramic earthenware decorated with an opaque glaze

glyph • sculptured symbol or character

hieroglyphs • pictures representing words, parts of words, or sounds

Hittites • ancient civilization whose country bordered Egypt; enemy of the Egyptian people

"House of Life" • temple district where priests studied, taught, and practiced astronomy, writing, medicine, mathematics, law, and theology

ivory • material of animal tusks, especially of elephants

lapis lazuli • semiprecious stone known for its deep blue color

malachite • bright green mineral used for ornaments

mummy • body of a person or an animal embalmed for burial

natron • kind of salt found in dried-up lake beds

necropolis • cemetery

papyrus • writing material made from the stem of the papyrus plant

pylon • a monumental structure that flanks the entranceway to a building

pyramid • Egyptian building with a square base and sloping sides meeting in a point

resin • natural substance used in the mummification process

ritual • ceremony

sarcophagus • stone coffin, often with sculptures or writing on it

scribe • person who writes out documents

tomb • area dug out in earth or carved from rock to contain a dead body

vaulted • arched

viziers • Pharaoh's top officials who oversee everyday life in Egypt

INDEX

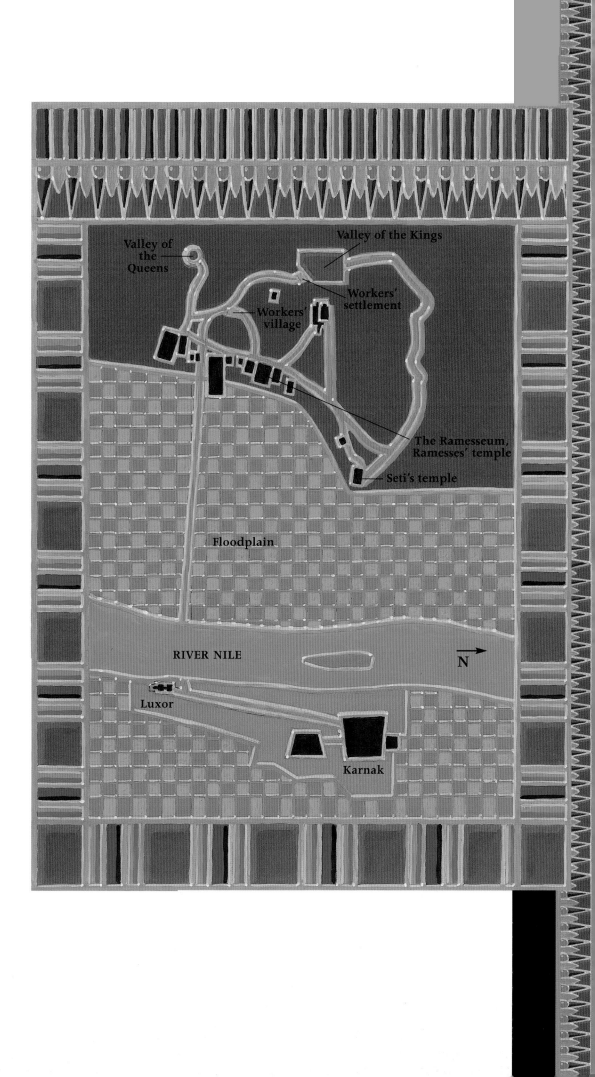

Valley of
the
Queens

Valley of the Kings

Workers'
settlement

Workers'
village

The Ramesseum,
Ramesses' temple

Seti's temple

Floodplain

RIVER NILE

N

Luxor

Karnak